6

www.pegasusforkids.com

© **B. Jain Publishers (P) Ltd.** All rights reserved. No part of this book may be reproduced, stored in a retrieval system or transmitted, in any form or by any means, mechanical, photocopying, recording or otherwise, without any prior written permission of the publisher.

Published by Kuldeep Jain for B. Jain Publishers (P) Ltd., D-157, Sector 63, Noida - 201307, U.P.
Registered office: 1921/10, Chuna Mandi, Paharganj, New Delhi-110055

Printed in India

Contents

Chapter 1: Pattern Completion 5

Chapter 2: Coding-Decoding 11

Chapter 3: Mirror and Water Images 15

Chapter 4: Direction and Sense Test 23

Chapter 5: Puzzle Test 31

Chapter 6: Ranking, Alphabet Test and Logical
              Sequence of Words 35

Answer Key 39

Preface

Logical Reasoning is an interesting and innovative series of six books, which will enhance the thinking skill of a child. This series will sharpen a child's mind and by practising the questions on regular basis, the child's brain will undergo a mental workout.

The presentation and the progressive learning process of the series makes solving the questions an enjoyable experience. A student develops a habit of thinking logically with daily practice. The series also strengthens the mental mathematics skills and help children to solve textbook level maths effortlessly. The questions are well-supported by icons, cartoon characters, and illustrations, making the series fascinating.

Each book has six chapters that focus on different aspects of thinking and make learning an easy and engrossing process. The various fascinating chapters include:

- Pattern completion
- Measuring units
- Geometrical shapes
- Grouping
- Ranking test
- Puzzle test
- Direction sense
- Time and calendar
- Coding-decoding
- Water and mirror images, etc.

We wind up this series with the hope that students, teachers and parents will appreciate our efforts and the students will practise the questions regularly. We invite constructive feedback for improvement of our future editions.

Pattern Completion

Choose the correct option in each of the following questions:

1. How many black triangles will be there in pattern 51?

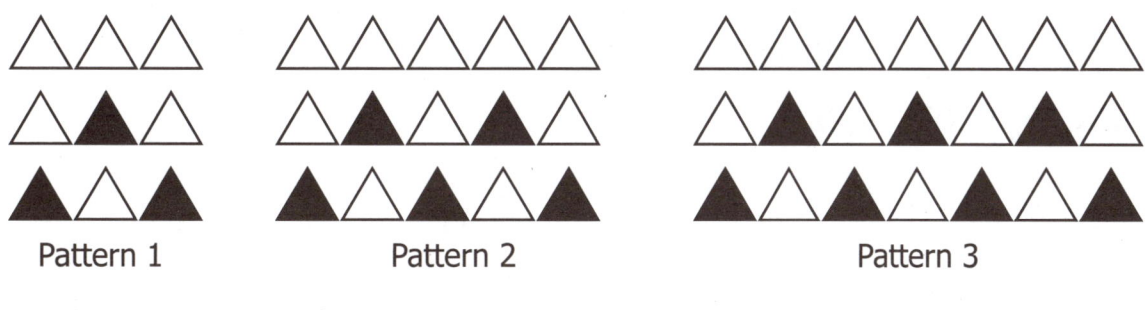

Pattern 1   Pattern 2   Pattern 3

a. 105   b. 103   c. 102   d. 104

2. Which pattern is the fourth in the series?

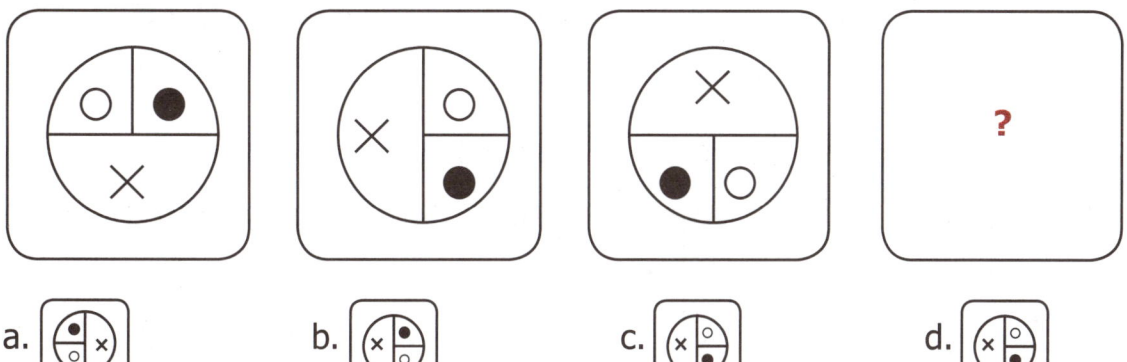

a.   b.   c.   d.

3. Which number is missing in the following series?

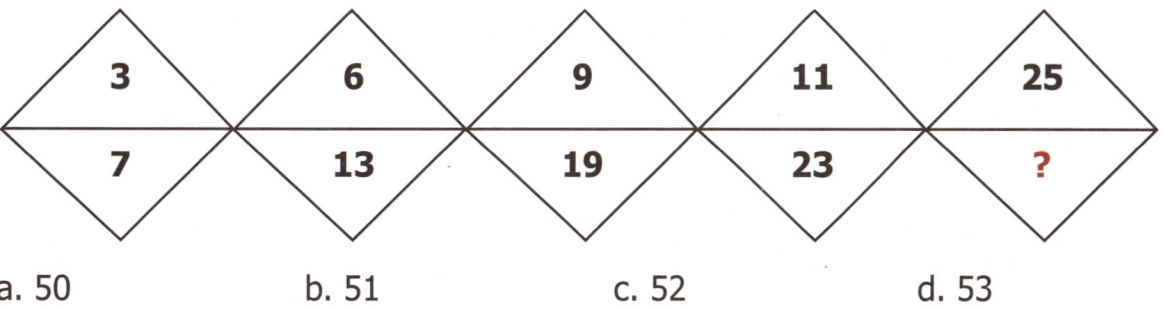

a. 50   b. 51   c. 52   d. 53

4. Which is the missing number in the number matrix?

10	20	8
12	?	10
6	0	10

a. 8 b. 10 c. 12 d. 14

5. Find the missing combination in the series given below:

FAG, GAH, HAI, IAJ, ………

a. JAK b. HAL c. HAK d. JAI

6. Find the missing combination in the series below:

ZA_5, Y_6B, XC_7, W_8D, ?

a. E_7V b. V_2E c. VE_5 d. VE_9

7. Find the missing number:

(stars containing: 1, 4, 9, 16, 25, ?, 49)

a. 36 b. 35 c. 40 d. 42

8. Which number will be the next in the series?

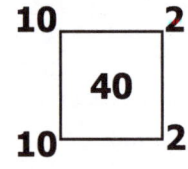 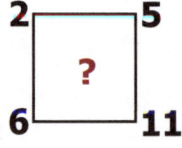

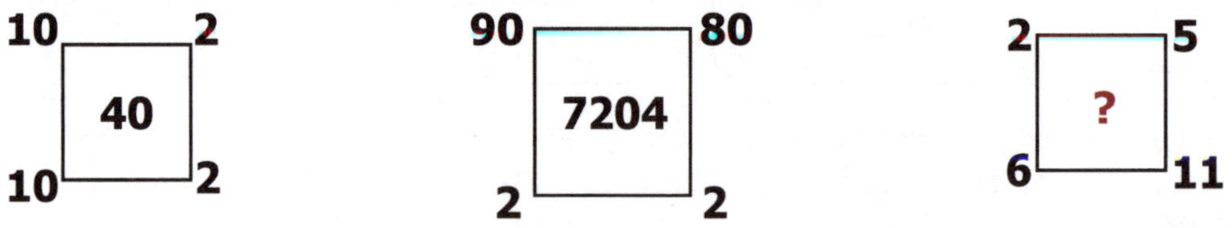

a. 77 b. 67 c. 76 d. 55

9. Which number will replace (?) in the given number pattern?

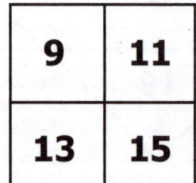

1	3
5	7

9	11
13	15

17	?
21	23

a. 19 b. 20 c. 25 d. 22

10. Look at the series given below and tick the number that should come next:

    53, 53, 40, 40, 27, 27, ?

    a. 12   b. 14   c. 27   d. 53

11. How many squares will be there in pattern 8?

    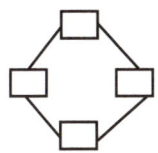 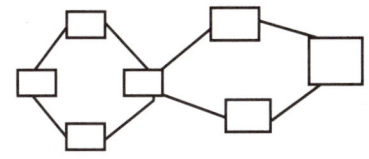 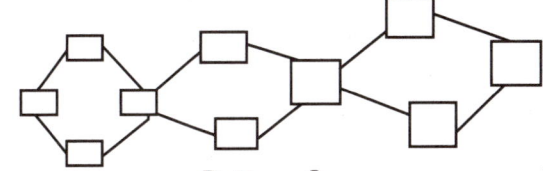

    Pattern 1   Pattern 2   Pattern 3

    a. 24   b. 25   c. 27   d. 31

12. Find the missing figure:

    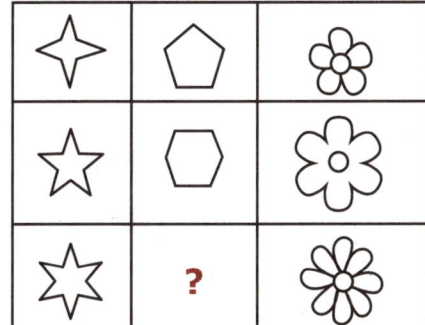

    a.    b.    c.    d.

13. Which number will replace (**?**) in the following number series?

    5   20   80   320   ?

    a. 1200   b. 1280   c. 1320   d. 1360

14. Fill the missing number in the pattern given below:

    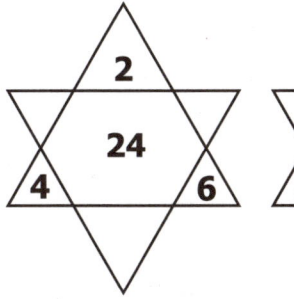 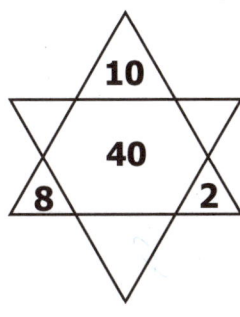 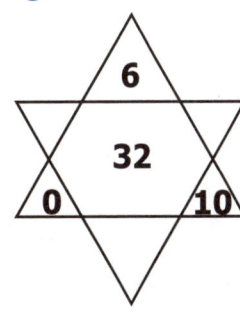 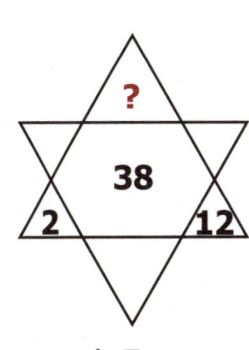

    a. 2   b. 4   c. 5   d. 7

15. Which of the following options will replace the (?)?

    a.   b.   c.   d.

16. Which figure will replace the (?) in figure pattern?

    a.   b.   c.   d.

17. Which two numbers will replace the question marks in the number pattern given below?

    225   196   169   ?   121   100   81   64   ?

    a. 49, 144   b. 144, 49   c. 64, 144   d. 144, 64

18. Which figure will replace the question mark in the figure pattern given below?

    a.   b.   c.   d.

19. How many unit squares will there be in pattern 61?

    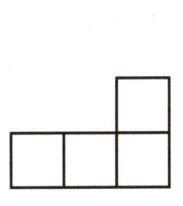   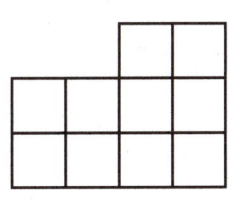   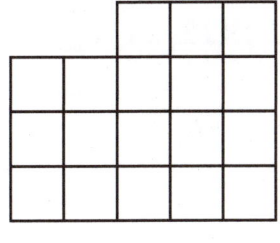   -------------------

    a. 3904   b. 4780   c. 3737   d. 8037

20. Which figure will replace the (?) in the figure?

    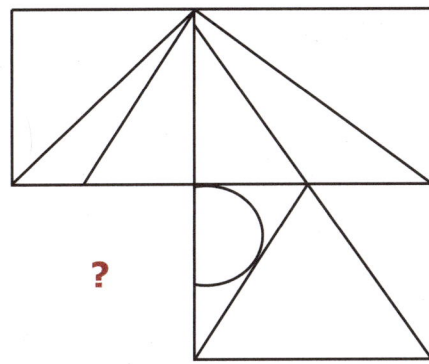

    a.   b.   c.   d.

21. Which shape should be placed in the blank space?

    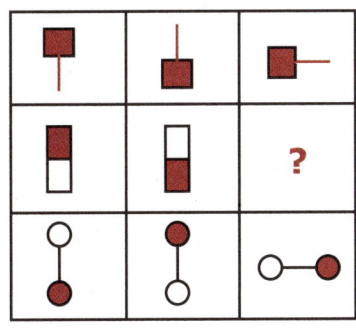

    a.   b.   c.   d.

22. What is the missing number in the following number pattern?

    | 5 | 20 | | 7 | 42 | | 9 | 72 | | 11 | ? |

    a. 115   b. 121   c. 111   d. 110

23. Find the missing combination in the series given below:

E5Z26, H8S20, N14K11, M_P_

a. 13, 16   b. 16, 13   c. 14, 13   d. 13, 14

24. Find the missing combination in the series given below:

ABCZYX, DEFWVU, GHITSR, ?

a. OPQJKL   b. JKLPQR   c. JKLQPO   d. RSTJKL

25. Which is the missing figure?

 a.    b.    c.    d.

2 Coding-Decoding

Coding is a method of expressing something in secret. Decoding is a process to understand a code language.

Choose the correct option in each of the following questions:

1. If CHINA is coded as 24681 and INDIGO is coded as 683659, then how will INDIA be coded?

    a. 68361   b. 68362   c. 28663   d. 28366

2. If the code of FLOWER is REWOLF, then how will the word DIVISION be coded?

    a. SIONIVID   b. VIDINOIS   c. NOISIVID   d. SIVIDNOI

3. If in a certain code 24685 is written as 35796, how will 35741 be written in the same code?

    a. 46852   b. 44826   c. 44880   d. 46682

4. If in a certain language PRESENT is coded as TNESERP and PAPER is coded as REPAP, then what will be the code of JANUARY?

    a. UNYRAA   b. YRAUNAJ   c. UNAJYRA   d. YRAAUN

5. If in a certain language GARIMA is coded as 234563 and REENA as 47713, how will REEMA be coded?

    a. 47376   b. 47736   c. 46637   d. 47763

6. Which figure has four equal sides if △ is called ▭, ▭ is called ◯, ◯ is called ☐, ☐ is called ◇, ◇ is called ✦ and ✦ is called ⬠?

   a. ◇   b. ▭   c. ☐   d. ✦

7. If Chair is called Table, Table is called Furniture, Furniture is called Desk, Desk is called Almirah, Almirah is called Bench, and Bench is called Bed, then where are the clothes kept?

   a. Furniture   b. Table   c. Desk   d. Bench

8. If PENCIL is written as NEPLIC, then how will BROKEN be written in the same code?

   a. ORBNEK   b. NEKORB   c. RBONEK   d. ONEKRB

9. If FOREST is written as ROFTSE, then how will AFRICA be written in the same code?

   a. ACARFA   b. ARACFA   c. RFAACI   d. ACFAAR

10. If GREEN is coded as 21557 and PARROT is coded as 601148, then how will REPEAT be coded?

    a. 565081   b. 156508   c. 508156   d. 815650

11. If WATER is coded as 91836 and CHAIR is coded as 57154, then how will WATCH be coded?

    a. 91857   b. 857189   c. 718589   d. 189857

12. If Butter is called Cheese, Cheese is called Cake, Cake is called Vegetable, Vegetable is called Flour and Flour is called Flower, then what is made from wheat?

    a. Flower   b. Flour   c. Cheese   d. Vegetable

13. If SYSTEM is coded as METSYS and FARTHER is coded as REHTRAF, then what is the code of NUMBER?

    a. ERNUMB   b. NUMREB   c. REBMUN   d. BNUREM

14. In a certain code, GIGANTIC is written as GIGTANCI. How is MIRACLES written in that code?

    a. MIRLACSE   b. ACSEMIRL   c. SEMIASRL   d. MIASRLSE

15. If Train is called Bus, Bus is called Tractor, Tractor is called Car, Car is called Scooter, Scooter is called Bicycle, and Bicycle is called Rickshaw, then which vehicle is used to plough a field?

    a. Bus   b. Car   c. Train   d. Tractor

16. If Road is called Rain, Rain is called Water, Water is called Cloud, Cloud is called Sky, Sky is called Sea and Sea is called Path, then where does ship sail?

    a. Rain   b. Road   c. Sea   d. Path

17. If PAPER is written as RCRGT, TRACTOR is written as VTCEVQT then SCHOOL will be written as _____.

    a. TDIPMM   b. UEKQNN   c. UEJQQN   d. UEJQMM

18. If Red is called Blue, Blue is called White, White is called Yellow, Yellow is called Green, Green is called Black, Black is called Violet, and Violet is called Orange, then what would be the colour of human blood?

    a. Red   b. Blue   c. Violet   d. Green

19. If ▢ means ▦, ▦ means ⊞, ⊞ means ◈, then which figure has exactly 10 squares?

    a. ◈   b. ⊞   c. ▢   d. ▦

20. If in a certain code language, BOARD is written as $3%#6 and ROPE is written as #35@, then PEAR will be written as _____.

    a. 5@%#   b. 5%6#   c. #6%5   d. 5X6%

21. If SHALLY is coded as BDNCCZ then LYSAH will be coded as _____.

    a. CZBND   b. CBZND   c. ZBNDB   d. DBNCZ

22. If 🌧 is called ☂, ☂ is called 🌈, 🌈 is called 🧥 and 🧥 is called ☁ then which among them is a piece of clothing?

    a. 🧥   b. 🌈   c. ☁   d. ☂

23. IF HINDUSTAN is coded as 592187462 and INDIA is coded as 92196 then how will HINDIA be coded?

    a. 219659   b. 592196   c. 699251   d. 152996

24. If TRAIN is coded as 97158 and TRACTOR is coded as 9712967 then how will IRON be coded?

    a. 9767   b. 9758   c. 5768   d. 9876

25. If COVER is written as REVOC, TRAIN is written as NIART, SOUP is written as PUOS then how will SOURCE be written?

    a. ECRUOS   b. SOECRU   c. OUESCR   d. SCREOU

3 Mirror and Water Images

A mirror image is a reflection of a person in a mirror. This reflected image is different from the original image in terms of orientation. This means, the left side of a person becomes the right side of that person in the mirror image, it undergoes lateral inversion.

Look at the tables given below and observe the change in the orientation of the alphabets in the respective mirror images.

Mirror Images of Capital Letters

Letters	Mirror Images	Letters	Mirror Images	Letters	Mirror Images
A	A	J	L	S	Ƨ
B	ꓭ	K	ꓘ	T	T
C	Ɔ	L	⅃	U	U
D	ꓷ	M	M	V	V
E	Ǝ	N	И	W	W
F	ꓞ	O	O	X	X
G	ꓚ	P	ꟼ	Y	Y
H	H	Q	Ọ	Z	Ƹ
I	I	R	Я		

Mirror Images of Numbers 1-9

1	1
2	ꙅ
3	ꓱ
4	ꓞ
5	ꙅ
6	ꓯ
7	⦢
8	8
9	ꓯ

15

A water image is the reflection of an object in water. It is normally obtained by inverting the position of an object upside down. For example look at the image given below:

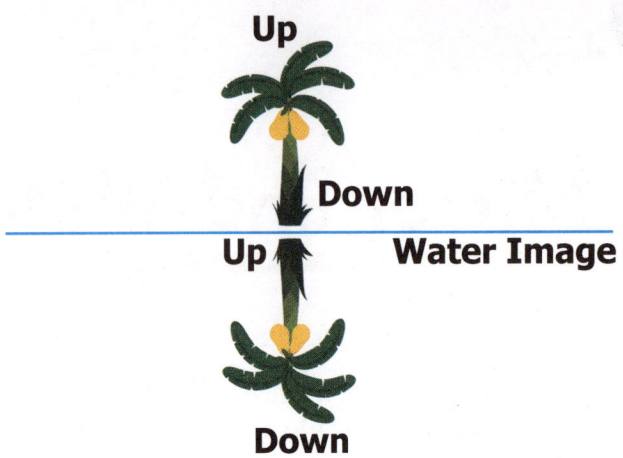

Water Images of Capital Letters

A	B	C	D	E	F	G	H	I
∀	B	C	D	E	F	G	H	I
J	K	L	M	N	O	P	Q	R
ſ	K	L	W	N	O	P	Q	R
S	T	U	V	W	X	Y	Z	-
S	⊥	∩	∧	M	X	⅄	Z	-

Water Images of Small Letters

a	b	c	d	e	f	g	h	i
ɐ	p	c	q	ɘ	ƚ	ɑ	ʜ	!
j	k	l	m	n	o	p	q	r
ꞁ	ʞ	l	ɯ	u	o	b	d	ɹ
s	t	u	v	w	x	y	z	-
s	ƚ	n	∧	w	x	ʎ	z	-

Water Images of Numbers

1 2 3 4 5 6 7 8 9
⇂ ट ε ߈ ϛ 6 ⌐ 8 6

(Direction: 1-10): Find the mirror images of the figures given below:

1.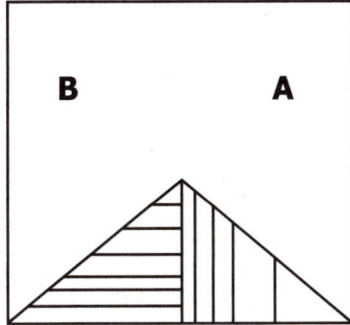

   a.    b.    c.    d.

2.

   a.   b.   c.   d.

3.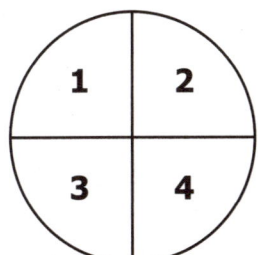

   a.   b.   c.   d.

4.

R	1
2	S

   a.   b.   c.   d.

5.

a.  b.  c.  d.

6. **REASON**

   a. REASON   b.  REASON (mirrored)   c.  NOSAER   d. REASON (vertical)

7.
     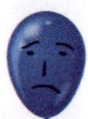

   a.    b.    c.    d.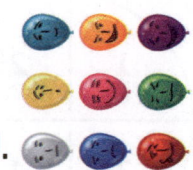

8.  ABCDEFG
   HIJKLM
   NOPQRST
   UVWXYZ

   a.    b. 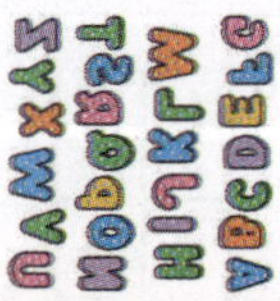   c.    d.

9.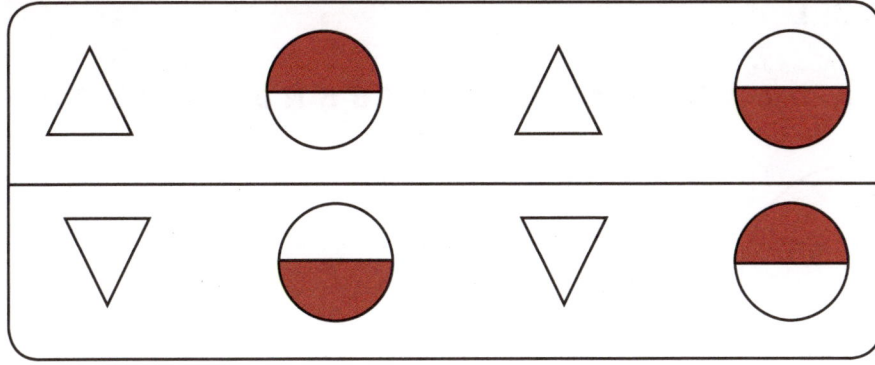

10.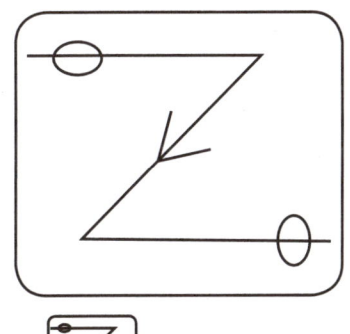

(Direction: 11-20): Find the water images of the figures given below:

11.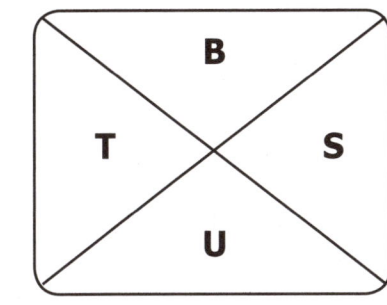

12.

a.    b.    c.    d.

13. **V T 5 6 B N 3 L**

a. L3NB65TV   b. VT56BN3L   c. VT56BN3L   d. L3NB65TV

14.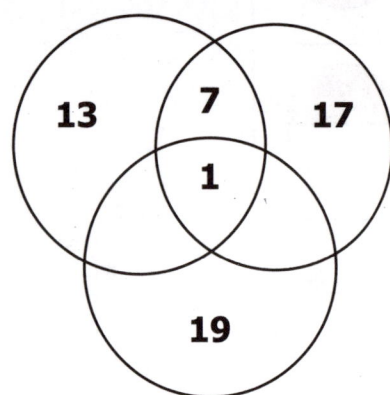

a. 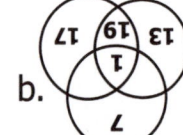   b. 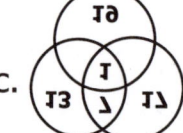   c. 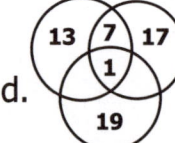   d. (13 7 17 / 1 / 19)

15.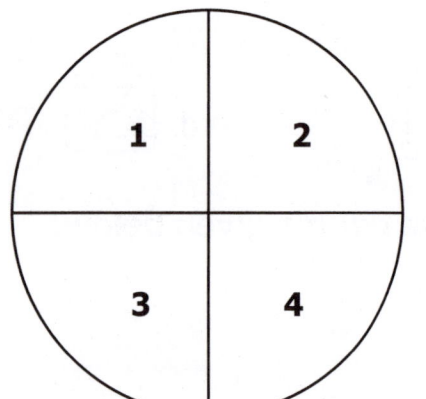

a.   b.   c.   d.

16.

a.    b.    c.    d.

17.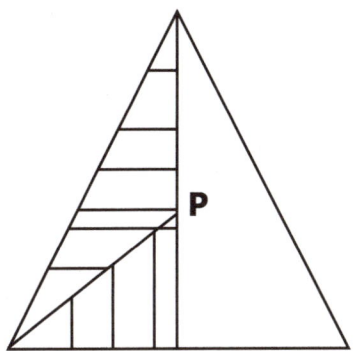

a.  b.  c.  d.

18. **E 1 B 2 N 5 S**

   a. S2N8I3   b. E1B2N5S   c. E1B2N5S   d. E1B2N5S

19.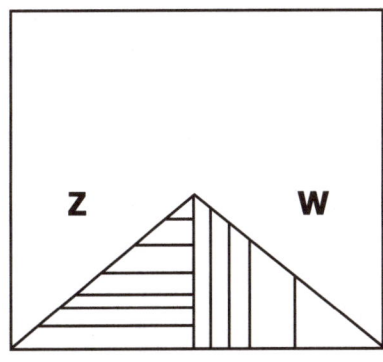

20. **1 A 6 B W 9**

   a. 1A6BW9   b. 1A6BW9   c. 1A6BW9   d. 9WB6A1

21. Find the mirror image of the figure given below:

22. Find the water image of the figure given below:

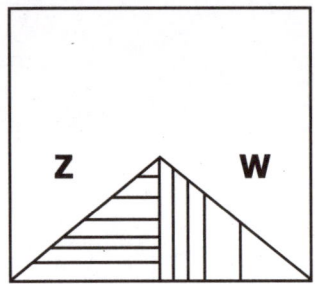

a.   b.   c.   d.

23. Find the mirror image of the clock given below:

a.   b.   c.   d.

24. Find the water image of the clock given below:

a.   b.   c.   d.

25. Find the mirror image of the figure given below:

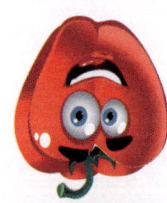

a.   b.   c.   d.

4 Direction and Sense Test

Such questions are designed to examine a child's knowledge related to sense of direction and movement of an object. Direction is a person's position with respect to another person, place or a thing. Look at the direction images given below. There are principally four directions (North, South, West and East) and four additional directions (North-west, North-east, South-west, South-east).

Directions

1.

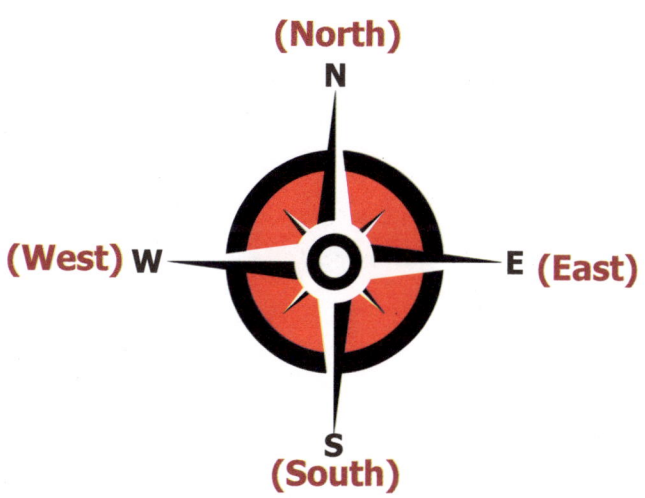

2.

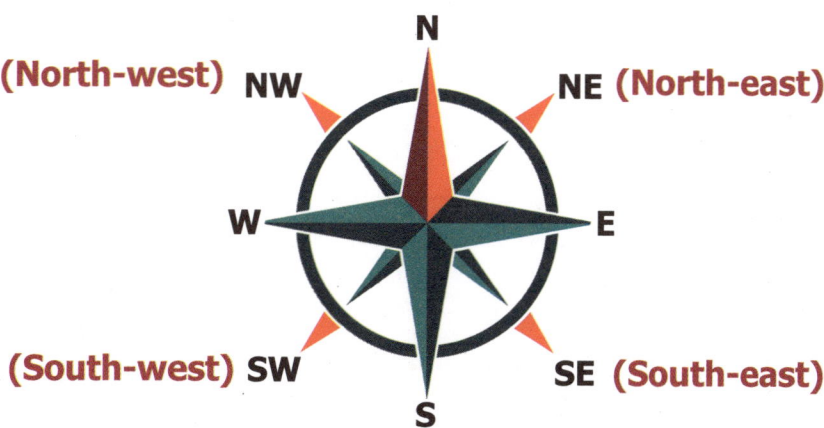

Angular Movement

Movement of an object in a curved or circular path is angular movement. Here the change of an object's position from initial to final state is shown in terms of angle. Observe the image given alongside to understand angular movement.

Clockwise Direction

When somebody moves in a direction which is same as the moving direction of a clock's hands, it is known as clockwise direction.

Anticlockwise Direction

Moving in the opposite direction of the clockwise direction is called anticlockwise direction.

Choose the correct option in each of the following questions:

1. Which point is north-west of S?

    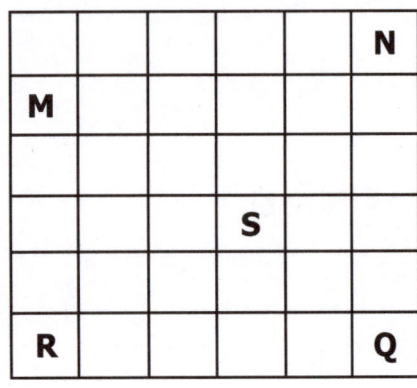

    a. M   b. N   c. Q   d. R

2. Which point is north-east of S?

    a. M   b. N   c. Q   d. R

3. If N and Q interchange their positions, what will be their new directions?

				N
M				
		S		
R				Q

a. north-east (N), south-east (Q)
b. south-east (N), north-east (Q)
c. south-west (N), south-east (Q)
d. north-west (N), north-east (Q)

4. Samuel is facing the library now. If he makes 270° turn to the right, he will be facing the _____.

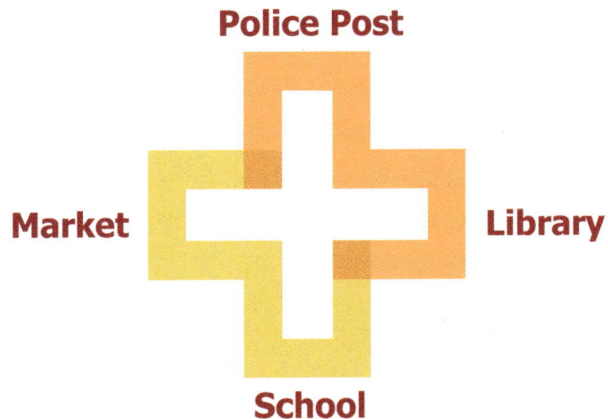

a. School   b. Market   c. Police Post   d. Library

5. Mark is going to school. He is facing the school now. After walking for 5 min, he takes a 90° right turn and then 45° right turn again. He will be facing _____.

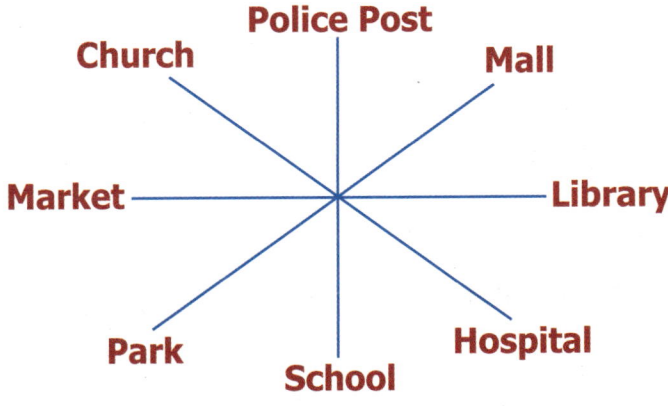

a. Church   b. Market   c. Library   d. Hospital

6. Johnny is facing the park. What will he be facing if he turns 315° clockwise?

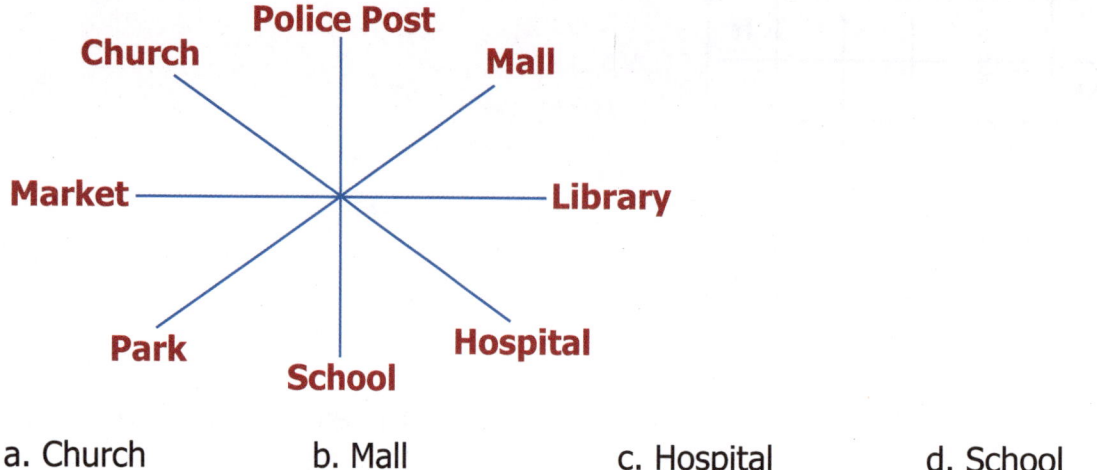

  a. Church   b. Mall   c. Hospital   d. School

7. Johnny is facing the park. What will he be facing if he turns 315° anticlockwise?

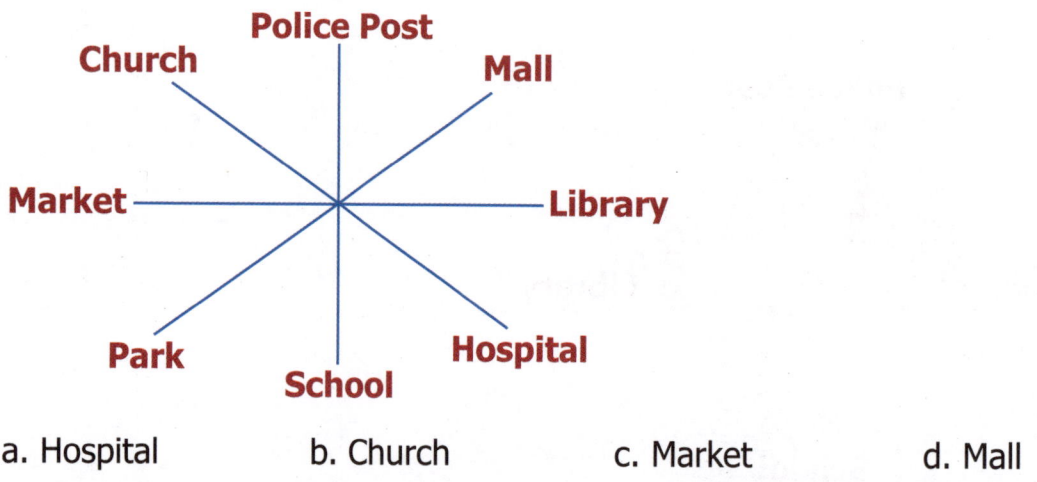

  a. Hospital   b. Church   c. Market   d. Mall

Direction (8-10): Study the given picture carefully and answer the following questions:

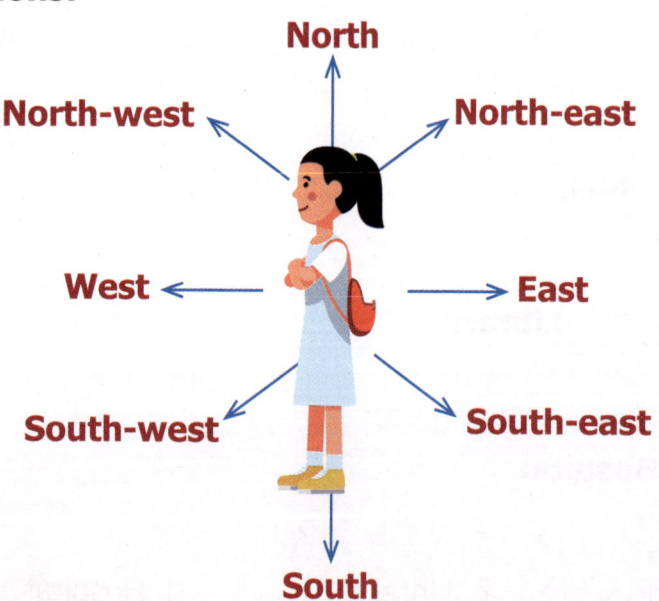

8. If the girl is facing east and turns 270° in a clockwise direction, in which direction will she be facing?

   a. west   b. north   c. south   d. south-west

9. If the girl is facing west and turn 270° in an anticlockwise direction, in which direction will she be facing?

   a. west   b. north   c. south   d. south-west

10. If the girl is facing south-west and turns in a clockwise direction to face north, what angle does she go through?

    a. 90°   b. 135°   c. 180°   d. 45°

11. Henry started from school, walked straight 2 km west, then turned left and walked straight 1 km, then again turned left and walked straight 5 km. In which direction is he now from his school?

    a. north   b. south   c. south-west   d. south-east

12. Jeff is facing the airport. What will he be facing, if he turns 315° anticlockwise?

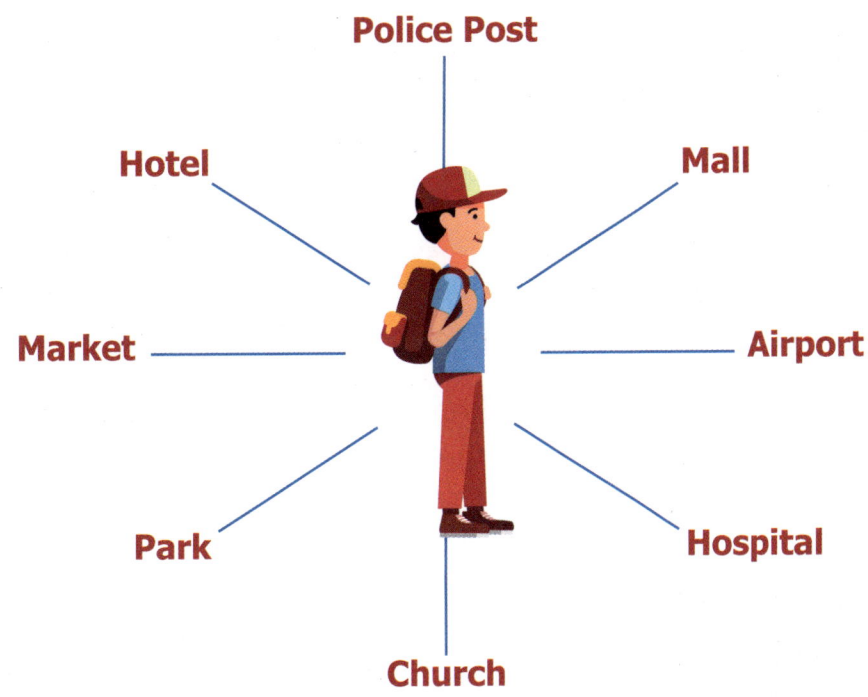

    a. Church   b. Hospital   c. Park   d. Market

13. Jeff is facing the airport. What will he be facing, if he turns 315° clockwise?

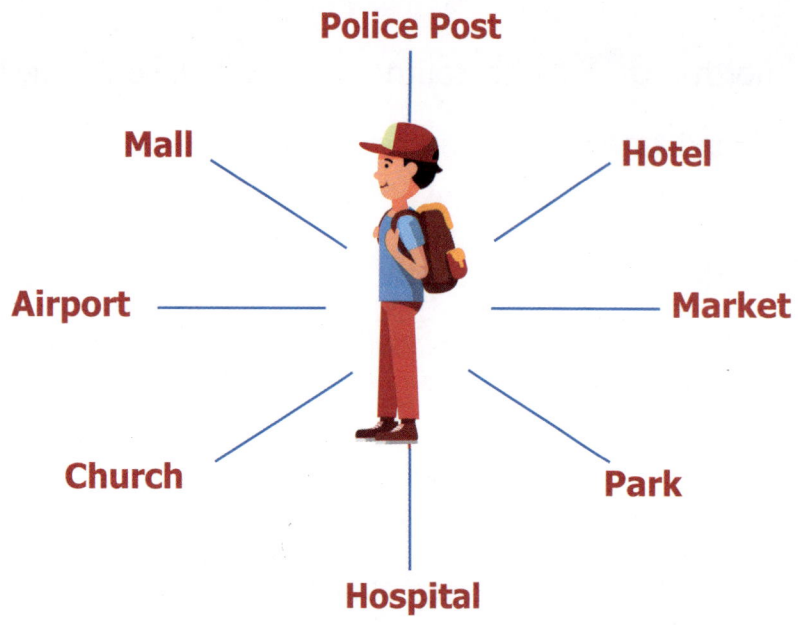

    a. Mall   b. Hospital   c. Park   d. Church

14. If the clock rotates 270° clockwise, then the hands will be in _____ direction.

    a. north   b. south   c. east   d. west

15. If the clock rotates 270° anticlockwise, then the hands will be in _____ direction.

    a. north   b. south   c. east   d. west

16. If the clock rotates 315° clockwise, then the hands will be in _____ direction.

    a. north-west   b. north-east   c. south   d. west

17. If the clock rotates 360° clockwise then the hands will be in _____ direction.

    a. north   b. south   c. east   d. west

18. P is facing pond. If he turns 180° clockwise and then 270° anticlockwise, then he will be facing _____.

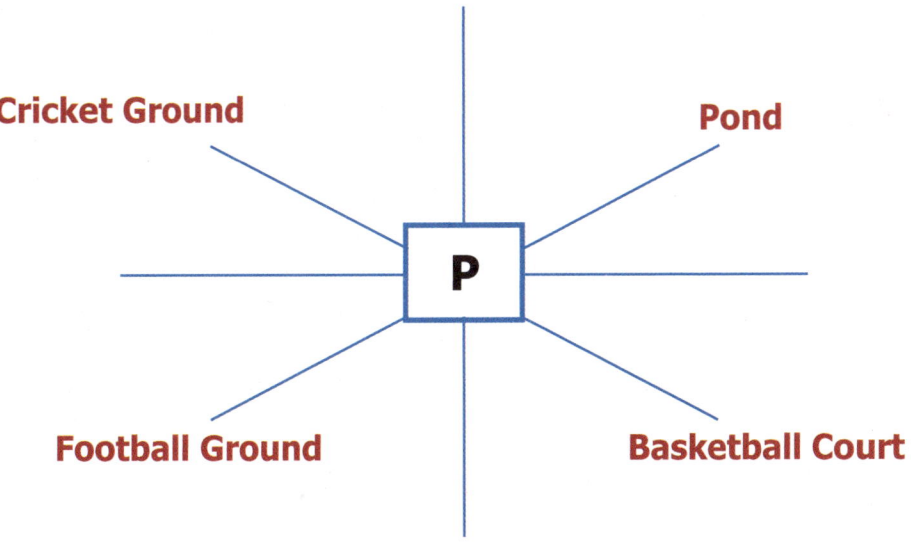

    a. Pond   b. Cricket Ground   c. Football Ground   d. Basketball Court

19. P is facing pond. If he turns 270° clockwise and then 180° anticlockwise, then he will be facing _____.

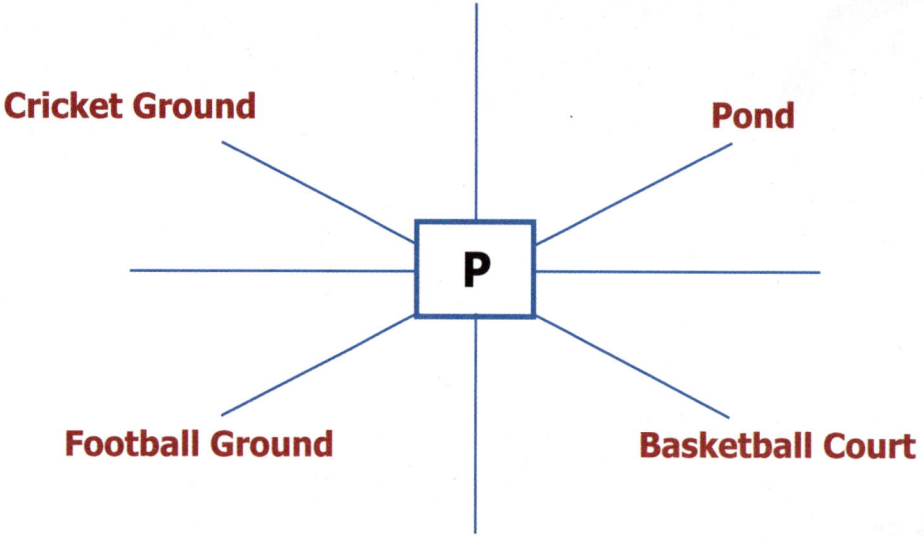

 a. Pond b. Football Ground c. Cricket Ground d. Basketball Court

20. P is facing football ground. If he turns 270° clockwise and then 180° anticlockwise, then he will be facing _____.

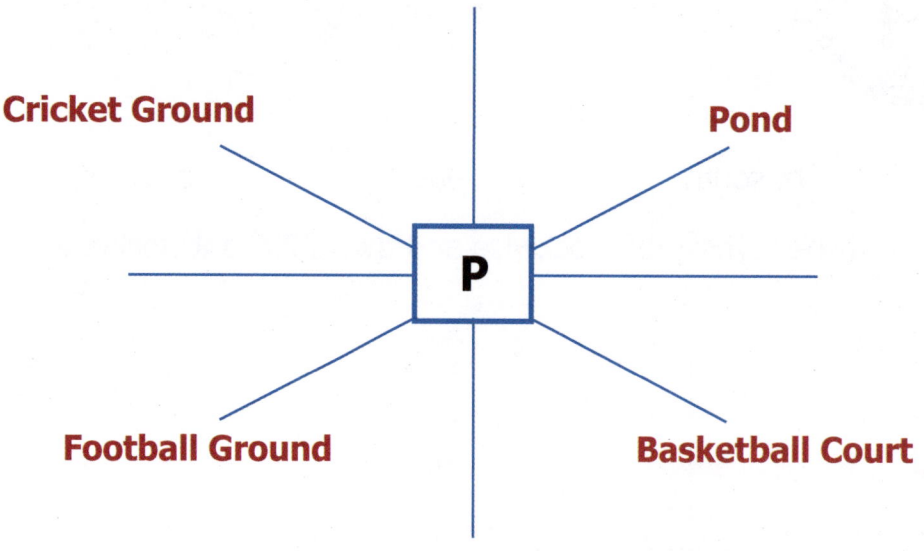

 a. Pond b. Football Ground c. Cricket Ground d. Basketball Court

5 Puzzle Test

Puzzle test is a concept-based brain game that makes kids smarter.

Choose the correct option in each of the following questions:

1. Ricky, Hamilton and Andy are good in Maths. Hamilton and Andy are good in Science and English. Ricky and Hamilton are good in Computers. James is good only in English. Find out who is good in all the subjects.

    a. Ricky   b. Hamilton   c. Andy   d. James

2. Rehana wrote down all the numbers from 1 to 100. Find out how many times she wrote 3:

    a. 10   b. 11   c. 20   c. 21

Direction (3-5): Read the following passage carefully and answer the questions given below:

Julia and Erin are good in chess and dance. Sophia and Julia are good in chess and singing. Olivia and Erin are good in dance and carom. Sophia, Olivia and Lily are good in singing and drawing.

3. Who among all is good in chess and singing?

    a. Julia   b. Erin   c. Sophia   d. Olivia

4. Who among all is good in chess, dance and carom?

    a. Julia   b. Erin   c. Sophia   d. Olivia

5. Who among all is not good in drawing?

    a. Sophia   b. Olivia   c. Lily   d. Julia

Direction (6-8): Read the following passage carefully and answer the questions given below:

There is a group of five boys. They are standing in a height wise manner. Now read the description.

    a. Joseph is second tallest
    b. James is taller than William and shorter than Joseph
    c. David is the tallest
    d. Oliver is shorter than William

6. Who is the shortest?

    a. Joseph   b. William   c. James   d. Oliver

7. Who is taller than Joseph?

    a. Oliver   b. David   c. William   d. James

8. Who is shorter than David but taller than James?

    a. Joseph   b. William   c. David   d. James

Read the direction in the following passage carefully and answer the questions (9-10):

Five girls took part in an educational competition. Results were as follows.

Emma scored less than Isabella but more than Olivia. Carroll scored more than Lily but less than Isabella. Olivia scored less than Carroll and Lily too.

9. Who scored maximum?

    a. Emma   b. Olivia   c. Isabella   d. Carroll

10. Who scored minimum?

    a. Emma   b. Olivia   c. Isabella   d. Carroll

11. Find P + Q + R + S, so that the sum of the numbers along each line is 12.

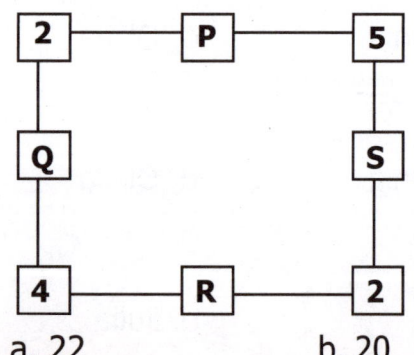

    a. 22   b. 20   c. 28   d. 30

12. Find P + Q + R + S, so that the sum of the numbers along each line is 15:

    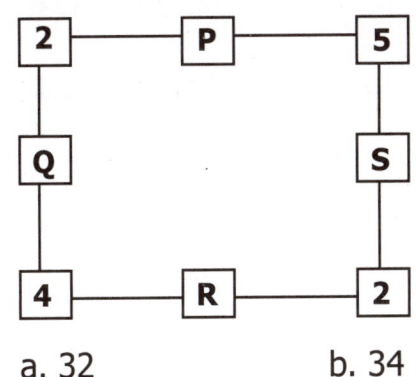

    a. 32 b. 34 c. 36 d. 38

Direction (13-15): Read the following information carefully and answer the questions given below:

Oliver celebrates his birthday on second Friday of **June 2016**.

13. The date after Oliver's birthday will be _____.

    a. 17 b. 9 c. 10 d. 11

14. Which date and day will it be after 5 days of his birthday?

    a. Thursday, 17 b. Friday, 17 c. Thursday, 16 d. Friday, 16

15. The day and date before Oliver's birthday was _____.

    a. Thursday, 9 b. Thursday, 11 c. Friday, 9 d. Friday, 11

16. A, J, M, P, Q and S are sitting in a row. Q and S are in the centre, and A and J are at the ends, M is sitting on the left of A. Then who is sitting on the right of J?

    a. A b. P c. J d. Q

17. Maddy wrote down all the numbers from 1 to 100. Find out how many times he wrote 0:

    a. 10 b. 11 c. 20 c. 21

Direction (18-19): Read the following information carefully and answer the questions given below:

Sam is taller than Rinni but shorter than Julia. Rinni is shorter than Anne but taller than Rehana. Julia is taller than Sam but shorter than Anne.

18. Who among them is the shortest?

    a. Rehana   b. Anne   c. Rinni   d. Julia

19. Who among them is the tallest?

    a. Rehana   b. Anne   c. Rinni   d. Julia

20. In how many ways can we form the word PAPER from the network shown?

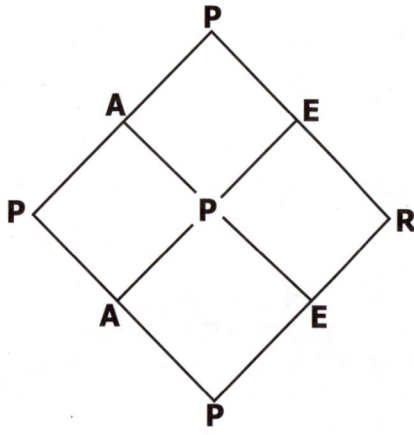

    a. 1   b. 2   c. 5   d. more than 5

6 Ranking, Alphabet Test and Logical Sequence of Words

Choose the correct option in each of the following questions:

1. Genelia ranked 8th in a class of 52 students from the top. What is her rank from the bottom in the class?

    a. 49th b. 48th c. 44th d. 43rd

2. In class 5th, Henry scored more than Bosco. Louis scored as much as Philip. Robert scored less than Jude. Bosco scored more than Louis. Jude scored less than Philip. Find out who scored the lowest.

    a. Henry b. Louis c. Philip d. Robert

3. Arrange the words in a meaningful logical order and then select the appropriate sequences from the options provided below:

    i. Locality ii. Family iii. Community iv. Member

    v. Country

    a. v, iv, iii, ii, i b. iv, ii, iii, i, v c. iii, i, ii, iv, v d. v, iii, i, iv, ii

4. Among, 1, 2, 3 and 4, 2 is heavier than 1 and 3. 3 is not as heavy as 1. 4 is heavier than 2. Who is the heaviest?

    a. 1 b. 2 c. 3 d. 4

5. Arrange the following words as they appear in a dictionary:

    i. Asia ii. Africa iii. Australia iv. America

    v. Afghanistan

    a. v, ii, iv, i, iii b. iii, iv, i, ii, v c. iv, i, ii, iii, v d. ii, iii, iv, i, v

6. Which of the following cannot be formed from the letters of the given word?

   ATTRIBUTABLE

   a. ATTITUDE   b. BATTER   c. EAT   d. TRIAL

7. Elliot ranked 15th in his class of 39 students from the bottom. What is his rank from the top?

   a. 25th   b. 26th   c. 24th   d. 23rd

8. Austin ranked 12th in his class of 63 students from the top. What is his rank from the bottom?

   a. 53rd   b. 52nd   c. 51st   d. 50th

9. Austin ranked 12th in his class from the top and Justin ranked 15th from the bottom in their class of 35 students. How many students are there between Austin and Justin?

   a. 6   b. 7   c. 8   d. 9

10. Which letter will be the 5th from right if 1st and 2nd, 3rd and 4th and so on are interchanged in the word COMPANION?

    a. O   b. I   c. A   d. N

11. Which letter will be the 6th from left if 1st and 2nd, 3rd and 4th and so on are interchanged in the word CIRCUMLOCUTION?

    a. M   b. U   c. C   d. L

12. Study the letter-number sequence given below carefully:

    B 3 K G 5 P D 7 9 E R J I M T 6 Z H Q 3 W 2 A

    Which of the following letter/number is exactly in the middle between the 9th letter/number from the left end and 7th letter/number from the right end?

    a. J   b. I   c. M   d. R

13. Study the letter-number-symbol sequence given below carefully:

    M4ET%J9IB@U8$N#F1V7*2AH3Y5!6K

    Which of the following letter/number/symbol is 19th from the left and right end of the above arrangement?

    a. @ and F   b. F and @

    c. U, and 7   d. 7 and U

Direction (14-15): Arrange the following words in each question in a logical sequence:

14. i. Evening
    ii. Morning
    iii. Night
    iv. Afternoon

    a. i, ii, iii, iv   b. ii, iii, iv, i   c. ii, iv, i, iii   d. i, ii, iv, iii

15. i. Birth
    ii. Child
    iii. School
    iv. Job
    v. Education

    a. i, ii, iii, v, iv   b. v, iv, iii, ii, i   c. iii, ii, iv, v, i   d. iv, v, i, ii, iii

16. Which word cannot be formed from the letters of the given word?

    DISTURBANCE

    a. BANK   b. DISTANCE   c. BAND   d. TURBAN

17. Which word can be formed from the letters of the given word?

    TECHNOLOGY

    a. LONGEST   b. LONELY   c. ECOLOGY   d. ALONG

Direction (18-20): Read the following information carefully and answer the questions given below:

Some letters in each of the following questions are given which are numbered 1, 2, 3, 4 and 5 followed by four alternatives containing combinations of these numbers. Find combination of numbers so that the letters form a meaningful word.

18. E   E   T   I   L
     5   1   3   4   2

   a. 1, 2, 4, 3, 5   b. 2, 4, 3, 5, 1   c. 1, 2, 4, 5, 3   d. 4, 5, 1, 2, 3

19. E   A   L   S   T
     1   2   3   4   5

   a. 2, 4, 5, 1, 3   b. 3, 1, 2, 4, 5   c. 5, 1, 3, 2, 4   d. 3, 2, 4, 5, 1

20. O   S   U   H   T
     1   2   3   4   5

   a. 3, 5, 4, 1, 2   b. 4, 1, 2, 3, 5   c. 1, 2, 3, 4, 5   d. 2, 1, 3, 5, 4

21. Which of the following cannot be formed from the letters of the given word?

   HOROSCOPE

   a. HOPE   b. COPE   c. HORSE   d. POP

22. Arrange the following words as they are appear in a dictionary.

   1. India   2. Indonesia   3. Iran   4. Iraq
   5. Ireland   6. Israel   7. Italy

   a. 1, 2, 3, 4, 5, 6, 7   b. 7, 6, 5, 4, 3, 2, 1
   c. 4, 5, 2, 1, 6, 7   d. 2, 1, 3, 4, 5, 6, 7

Answer Key

Chapter 1

1. b	2. a	3. b	4. a	5. a	6. d
7. a	8. c	9. a	10. b	11. b	12. d
13. b	14. c	15. d	16. a	17. b	18. c
19. a	20. c	21. a	22. d	23. a	24. c
25. b					

Here are some hints to help you with the answers:

1. Pattern followed: (1 x 2) + 1, (2 x 2) + 1, (3 x 2) + 1, ...
   Number of shaded triangle in Pattern 51 = 51 x 2 + 1 =

3. In these boxes, pattern followed is Q = P x 2 + 1
   So, 25 x 2 + 1 = 51

4. Column wise the sum of the numbers in each column is 28.

5. Letters at the middle are static. Concentrate on the first and the third letters. Series involves an alphabetical order with repetition of third letter as the first of another in sequence.

6. There are 3 series to look for here. The first letters are alphabetical in reverse Z, Y, X, W, V. Second letters are in alphabetical order beginning with A. Third is the number series as 5, 6, 7...

7. (1 + 3 = 4, 4 + 5 = 9, 9 + 7 = 16, 16 + 9 = 25, 25 + 11 = 36, 36 + 13 = 49, Each digit is added with the consecutive odd number.

8.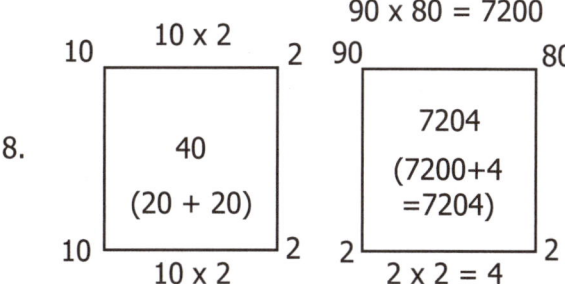

10. Each number is repeated, then 13 is subtracted to arrive at the next number.
14. (2 + 6 + 4) x 2 = 24, (10 + 8 + 2) x 2 = 40, (6 + 10 + 0) x 2 = 32, (12 + 2 + 5) x 2 = 38
17. Each number is the square of numbers from 15 in decreasing order
    15 x 15 = 225, 14 x 14 = 196
19. Pattern followed:
    Number of rows 2 x Number of columns 3 - 2 = Number of unit squares
    Pattern 1:
    2 x 3 -2 = 4
    So, pattern 61 = 62 x 63 – 2 = 3,904
22. Pattern followed:
    5 x 5 = 25 -5 = 20, 7 x 7 = 49 – 7 = 42, 9 x 9 = 81 – 9 = 72, 11 x 11 = 121 – 11 = 110

23. Pattern followed:
    Alphabet then its order number in alphabet series
24. Pattern followed: Three letters from starting and three from last

Chapter 2

1. a	2. c	3. a	4. b	5. d	6. a
7. d	8. a	9. c	10. b	11. a	12. a
13. c	14. a	15. b	16. d	17. c	18. b
19. d	20. a	21. a	22. b	23. b	24. c
25. a					

Here are some hints to help you with the answers:

2. Reverse spelling.
3. In new code every digit in the number is one more than its respective digit in the given number.
4. Letters of the word are written in reverse order.
17. Each letter is written two letters forward.

Chapter 3

1. a	2. c	3. d	4. a	5. b	6. a
7. a	8. d	9. a	10. d	11. c	12. b
13. b	14. c	15. a	16. d	17. c	18. b
19. a	20. b	21. b	22. d	23. c	24. a
25. b					

Chapter 4

1. a	2. b	3. b	4. c	5. a	6. d
7. c	8. b	9. b	10. b	11. d	12. b
13. a	14. d	15. c	16. a	17. a	18. b
19. d	20. c				

Chapter 5

1. b	2. c	3. a	4. b	5. d	6. d
7. b	8. a	9. c	10. b	11. a	12. b
13. d	14. c	15. a	16. b	17. b	18. a
19. b	20. d				

Chapter 6

1. c	2. d	3. b	4. d	5. a	6. a
7. c	8. c	9. c	10. d	11. b	12. b
13. d	14. c	15. a	16. a	17. c	18. a
19. b	20. d	21. d	22. a		